HORSES WITHOUT GRASS

*How We Kept Six Horses Moving and Eating
Happily & Healthily on an Acre and
a Half of Rock and Dirt*

Published in the United States by 14 Hands Press,
an imprint of Camp Horse Camp, LLC
www.14handspress.com
Some of the material herein has appeared
in other books by Joe Camp
Library of Congress subject headings
Camp, Joe
Horses Without Grass / by Joe Camp
Horses
Human-animal relationships
Horses-health
Horsemanship
The Soul of a Horse: Life Lessons from the Herd
ISBN 978-1-930681-40-8
First Edition

HORSES WITHOUT GRASS

*How We Kept Six Horses Moving and Eating
Happily & Healthily on an Acre and
a Half of Rock and Dirt*

JOE CAMP

14 HANDS PRESS

Also by Joe Camp

The National Best Seller
The Soul of a Horse
Life Lessons from the Herd

The Highly Acclaimed Best Selling Sequel
Born Wild
The Soul of a Horse

Horses & Stress
Eliminating the Root Cause of Most Health, Hoof & Behavior Problems

Why Relationship First Works
Why and How It Changes Everything

Beginning Ground Work
Everything We've Learned About Relationship and Leadership

Training with Treats
*With Relationship and Basic Training Locked In Treats Can Be
an Excellent Way to Enhance Good Communication*

God Only Knows
Can You Trust Him with the Secret?

Why Our Horses Are Barefoot
*Everything We've Learned About the
Health and Happiness of the Hoof*

The Soul of a Horse Blogged
The Journey Continues

Horses Were Born To Be On Grass
*How We Discovered the Simple But Undeniable Truth About Grass, Sugar,
Equine Diet & Lifestyle*

Who Needs Hollywood
The Amazing Story of How Benji Became the #3 Movie of the Year

Dog On It
Everything You Need To Know About Life Is Right There At Your Feet

"Joe Camp is a master storyteller." - *THE NEW YORK TIMES*

"Joe Camp is a natural when it comes to understanding how animals tick and a genius at telling us their story. His books are must-reads for those who love animals of any species." - *MONTY ROBERTS, AUTHOR OF NEW YORK TIMES BEST-SELLER THE MAN WHO LISTENS TO HORSES*

"Camp has become something of a master at telling us what can be learned from animals, in this case specifically horses, without making us realize we have been educated, and, that is, perhaps, the mark of a real teacher. The tightly written, simply designed, and powerfully drawn chapters often read like short stories that flow from the heart." - *JACK L. KENNEDY, THE JOPLIN INDEPENDENT*

"One cannot help but be touched by Camp's love and sympathy for animals and by his eloquence on the subject." - *MICHAEL KORDA, THE WASHINGTON POST*

"Joe Camp is a gifted storyteller and the results are magical. Joe entertains, educates and empowers, baring his own soul while articulating keystone principles of a modern revolution in horsemanship." - *RICK LAMB, AUTHOR AND TV/RADIO HOST "THE HORSE SHOW"*

For Kathleen, who loved me enough to initiate all this
when she was secretly terrified of horses

C ONTENTS

INTRODUCTION

Often, in the early evening, when the stresses of the day are weighing heavy, I pack it in and head out to the pasture. I'll sit on my favorite rock, or just stand, with my shoulders slumped, head down, and wait. It's never long before I feel the magical tickle of whiskers against my neck, or the elixir of warm breath across my ear, a restoring rub against my cheek. I have spoken their language and they have responded. And my problems have vanished. This book is written for everyone who has never experienced this miracle.

- Joe Camp
The Soul of a Horse
Life Lessons from the Herd

1
HINDGUTS AND HOLLYWOOD

Our house came with a couple of horse stalls, both painted a crisp white, one of them covered with a rusty red roof. They were cute. Often, over the three years we had lived there, we could be found in the late afternoon sitting on our front porch, looking out over the stalls, watching the sun sink beneath the ridge of mountains to the west. One of us would say, "Those stalls surely seem empty." Or, "Wouldn't it be nice if there were a couple of horses ambling back and forth down in the stalls?"

Like a postcard.

A lovely picture at sunset.

With cute horse stalls.

Lesson #1: Cute horse stalls are not adequate reason to purchase three horses.

Never mind the six we own now.

We had no idea what we were getting into. No clue and, before that moment, no horses.

And no grass. Except around the front door. But that didn't matter because at the time we didn't know horses were born to be on grass and needed grass or some kind of grass forage passing through their hindgut at least eighteen hours a day.

Excuse me, hindgut? What the devil is that?

Like I said, no clue.

Two complete neophytes stumbling through this enigmatic world of horses trying to figure out why most of the things people were telling us to do seemed to make no sense whatsoever.

Why were we even asking questions? The answer to that, I think, is an important part of this journey, and important for you to understand from where our motivation was coming.

Not just important actually. Critical.

It began with a chance meeting with Monty Roberts. Well, not a *real* meeting. We were making the obligatory trip that new horse owners must make to Boot Barn when Kathleen picked up a *California Horse Trader.* As we sat around a table watching the kids chomp cheese burgers, she read an article about Monty and it quite simply changed my life forever.

This man is responsible for us beginning our relationship with horses as it *should* begin, with the relationship *first*, and propelling us onto a collision course with the discovery that there was something very wrong in this world of horses. A world that has reminded me that you cannot, in fact, tell a book by its cover; that no "expert" should ever be beyond question just because somebody somewhere has given him or her such a label. That everybody and everything is up for study. That logic and good sense still provide the most reasonable answers, and still, given exposure, will prevail.

My first encounter with this lesson was way back when I was making the original Benji movie, our very first motion picture.

On a trip from Dallas to Hollywood to interview film labs and make a decision about which one to use, I discovered that intelligent, conscientious, hardworking people can sometimes make really big mistakes because they don't ask enough questions, or they take something for granted, or, in some cases, they just want to take the easiest way. In this case it was about how our film was to be finished in the lab, and my research had told me that a particular method (we'll call it Method B) was the best way to go. Everyone at every lab I visited, without exception, said, *Oh no, no. Method A is the best way.* When asked why, to a person, they all said *Because that's the way it's always been done!* In other words, *don't rock the boat.*

Not good enough, says I. My research shows that Method B will produce a better finished product, and that's what we want.

Finally, the manager of one of the smaller labs I visited scratched his head and said, "Well, I guess that's why David Lean uses Method B."

I almost fell out of my chair. For you youngsters, David Lean was the director of such epic motion pictures as *Dr. Zhvivago* and *Lawrence of Arabia.* I had my answer. And, finally, I knew I wasn't crazy.

It's still a mystery to me how people can ignore what seems so obvious, so logical, simply because it would mean *change.* Even though the change is for the better. I say look forward to the opportunity to learn something new. Relish and devour knowledge with gusto. Always be reaching for the best possible way to do things. It keeps you alive, and healthy, and happy. And makes for a better world.

Just because something has *always been done* a certain way does not necessarily mean it's the best way, or the correct way, or the healthiest way for your horse, or your relationship with your horse, or your life. Especially if, after asking a few questions, the traditional way defies logic and good sense, and falls short on compassion and respect.

The truth is too many horse owners are shortening their horses' lives, degrading their health, and limiting their happiness by the way they keep and care for them.

But it doesn't have to be that way. Information is king. Gather it from every source, make comparisons, and evaluate results. And don't take just one opinion as gospel. Not mine or anyone else's. Soon you'll not only feel better about what you're doing, you'll do it better. And the journey will be fascinating.

We were only a year and a half into this voyage with horses as these words found their way into the computer, but it was an obsessive, compulsive year and a half, and the wonderful thing about being a newcomer is that you start with a clean plate. No baggage. No preconceptions. No musts. Just a desire to learn what's best for our horses, and our relationship with them. And a determination to use logic and knowledge wherever found, even if it means exposing a few myths about what does, in fact, produce the best results. In short, I'll go with Method B every time.

2
CHOICES

After Kathleen had read to me about Monty Roberts I went straight home and ordered his books and DVDs and that's how I came to find myself in a round pen three days later staring off our big new Arabian.

I remember that it was an unusually chilly day for late May, because I recall the jacket I was wearing. Not so much the jacket, I suppose, as the collar. The hairs on the back of my neck were standing at full attention, and the collar was scratching at them.

There was no one else around. Just me and this eleven-hundred pound creature I had only met once before. And today he was passing out no clues as to how he felt about that earlier meeting, or about me. His stare was without emotion. Empty. Scary to one who was taking his very first step into the world of horses.

If he chose to do so this beast could take me out with no effort whatsoever. He was less than fifteen feet away. No halter, no line. We were surrounded by a round pen a mere fifty feet in diameter. No place to hide. Not that he was mean. At least I had been told that he wasn't. But I had also been told that anything is possible with a horse. He's a prey animal, they had said. A freaky flight animal that can flip from quiet and thoughtful to wild and reactive in a single heartbeat. Accidents happen.

I knew very little about this horse, and none of it firsthand. Logic said do not depend upon hearsay. Be sure. There's nothing like firsthand knowledge. But all I knew was what I could see. He was big.

The sales slip stated that he was unregistered. And his name was Cash.

But there was something about him. A kindness in his eyes that betrayed the vacant expression. And sometimes he would cock his head as if he were asking a question. I wanted him to be more than chattel. I wanted a relationship with this horse. I wanted to begin at the beginning, as Monty Roberts had prescribed. *Start with a blank sheet of paper, then fill it in.*

Together.

I'm not a gambler. Certainty is my mantra. Knowledge over luck. But on this day I was gambling.

I had never done this before.

I knew dogs.

I did not know horses.

And I was going to ask this one to do something he had probably never been asked to do in his lifetime. To make a choice. Which made me all the more nervous. What if it didn't work?

What if his choice was not *me*?

Cash was pawing the ground, wondering, I suspect, why I was just standing there in the round pen doing nothing. The truth is I was reluctant to start the process. Nervous. Rejection is not one of my favorite concepts. Once started, I would soon be asking him to make his choice. What if he said no? Is that it? Is it over? Does he go back to his previous owner?

I have often felt vulnerable during my sixty-eight years, but rarely *this* vulnerable. I really *wanted* this horse to choose me.

What if I screw it up? Maybe I won't do it right. It's my first time. What if he runs over me? Actually, that was the lowest on my list of concerns because Monty's Join-Up process is built on the language of the horse, and the fact that the raw horse inherently perceives humans as predators. Their response is flight, not fight. It's as automatic as breathing.

Bite the bullet, Joe, I kept telling myself. Give him the choice.

I had vowed that this would be our path. We would begin our relationship with every horse in this manner. Our way to true horsemanship, which, as I would come to understand, was not about how well you ride, or how many trophies you win, or how fast your horse runs, or how high he or she jumps.

I squared my shoulders, stood tall, looked this almost sixteen hands of horse straight in the eye, appearing as much like a predator as I could muster, and tossed one end of a soft long-line into the air behind him, and off he went at full gallop around the round pen. Just like Monty said he would.

Flight.

I kept my eyes on his eyes, just as a predator would. Cash would run for roughly a quarter of a mile, just as horses do in the wild, before he would offer his first signal. Did he actually think I was a predator, or did he know he was being tested? I believe it's somewhere in between, a sort of leveling of the playing field. A starting from scratch with something he knows ever so well. Predators and flight. A simulation, if you will. Certainly he was into it. His eyes were wide, his nostrils flared. At the very least he wasn't sure about me, and those fifty-two million years of genetics were telling him to flee.

It was those same genetics that caused him to offer the first signal. His inside ear turned and locked on me, again as Monty had predicted. He had run the quarter of a mile that usually preserves him from most predators; and I was still there, but not really seeming very predatory. So now, instead of pure reactive flight, he was getting curious. Beginning to *think* about it. Maybe he was even a bit confused. Horses have two nearly separate brains. Some say one is the reactive brain and the other is the thinking brain. Whether or not that's true physiologically, emotionally it's a good analogy. When they're operating from the reactive side, the rule of thumb is to stand clear until you can get them thinking.

Cash was now shifting. He was beginning to think. *Hmm, maybe this human is not a predator after all. I'll just keep an ear out for a bit. See what happens.*

Meanwhile, my eyes were still on his eyes, my shoulders square, and I was still tossing the line behind him.

Before long, he began to lick and chew. Signal number two. *I think maybe it's safe to relax. I think, just maybe, this guy's okay. I mean, if he really wanted to hurt me, he's had plenty of time, right?*

And, of course, he was right. But, still, I kept up the pressure. Kept him running. Waiting for the next signal.

It came quickly. He lowered his head, almost to the ground, and began to narrow the circle. Signal number three. *I'll look submissive, try to get closer, see what happens. I think this guy might be a good leader. We should discuss it.*

He was still loping, but slower now. Definitely wanting to negotiate. That's when I was supposed to take my eyes off him, turn away, and lower my head and shoulders. No longer predatorial, but assuming a submissive stance of my own, saying *Okay, if it's your desire, come on in. I'm not going to hurt you. But the choice is yours.*

The moment of truth. Would he in fact do that? Would he make the decision, totally on his own, to come to me? I took a deep breath, and turned away.

He came to a halt and stood somewhere behind me.

The seconds seemed like hours.

"Don't look back," Monty had warned. "Just stare at the ground."

A tiny spider was crawling across my new Boot Barn boot. The collar of my jacket was tickling the hairs on the back of my neck. And my heart was pounding. Then a puff of warm, moist air brushed my ear. My heart skipped a beat. He was really close. Then I felt his nose on my shoulder... the moment of *Join-Up*. I couldn't believe it. Tears came out of nowhere and streamed down my cheeks. I had spoken to him in his own language, and he had listened... and he had chosen to be with me. He had said *I trust you.*

I turned and rubbed him on the face, then walked off across the pen. Cash followed, right off my shoulder, wherever I went.

Such a rush I haven't often felt.

And what a difference it has made as this newcomer stumbled his way through the learning process. Cash has never stopped trying, never stopped listening, never stopped giving.

And for that reason neither have I.

I made a promise to him that day that he would lead the very best life I could possibly give him.

It was a year and a half and a lot of research later before I even had a clue what kind of life that might be.

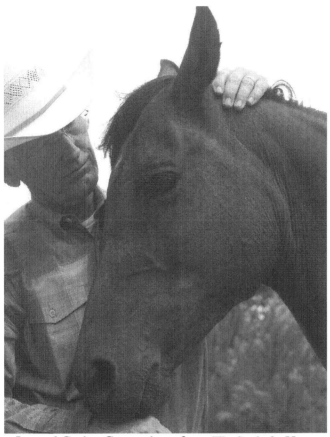

Joe and Cash – Cover photo from *The Soul of a Horse*

3
THE WILD HORSE MODEL

Our first three horses occupied those cute little stalls for almost a year. They all wore metal shoes, ate sugar-filled pellets from a table-high bucket, and hay from a feeder even further off the ground. They stood in one spot to eat their two meals a day with no reason to move around. In fact, they stood in one spot most of the day. They had nowhere to go. They *did* have time with the herd. Sort of. The three stalls were open to each other and the horse in the middle could actually nip or be nipped by the two who flanked him. Not because we set it up that way. That's how it was when we bought the house. Fortunately, there was no barn or I'm sure they would've been in it. But there were also no pastures or turnouts, and the only exercise the trio got was when we took them to our small arena. We bought leg wraps. Almost bought blankets. In short, we were the typical horse owners.

Almost.

But I couldn't turn loose of my promise to Cash. And the illogical answers we continued to receive about how the horses were supposed to be cared for and why. All of that continued to haunt me. So I began to spend almost as much time on the computer as I was spending with the horses. Kathleen says the real title of *The Soul of a Horse* should've been *Google It*. But the information I was uncovering was blowing me away.

Who knew that every horse on the planet is genetically the same? It's a scientific truth. Why, I wondered, did I not know this? And does it make any difference? Quite bit, I discovered.

To the horse.

Not too long after those first three horses had shown up in our front yard I stumbled into wild horse research trying to uncover why Cash had come to us with shoes on his front feet but none on his back feet. We had been told that concrete and asphalt would crack and shatter any horse's hoof that was not wearing a shoe. If that were true, I needed to get shoes on his back feet right now because we had concrete and asphalt everywhere.

And I suppose I had wondered – apparently too often too loud – how wild horses had managed to exist all this time without help from humans? Could it be the wild ones might be able to teach us a thing or two?

Oh no. Generations of selective breeding have completely changed everything about the domesticated horse.

That's when I happened upon Jaime Jackson's research on wild horses. And how well their hooves had protected them and helped them survive for millions of years.

And studies by Dr. Hiltrud Strasser, noted veterinarian, researcher, and author, who concluded that horses in the care of man have a life expectancy that is, for the most part, only a fraction of that of their wild-living counterparts. Usually because of problems with their locomotor organs. In other words, lameness.

Issues with their feet.

Caused by wearing metal shoes. And standing around all day in a tiny box stall. And eating sugar. Not from the ground. And stress.

Wow!

All followed by more digging, often leaving the horses in favor of science. Which ultimately lead to the mother lode which, in turn, began to unravel, uncover and assemble a list of undeniable truths. Facts so scientifically rock solid that there can be no basis for denial. To wit:

1. Science confirms that it would take a minimum of 5000 years – probably closer to 10,000 – to even begin to change the base genetics of *any*

species. In other words, a few hundred years of selective breeding has no effect on base genetics whatsoever. Which means that the domestic horse and the horse in the wild are genetically exactly the same. Everything begins with this.

2. DNA sequencing was performed on bones of horses discovered in the Alaskan permafrost dating 12,000 to 28,000 years ago and the results were compared to DNA sequencing from today's domestic horse. There was less than 1.2% difference between the two. Documented and on record. So, again, there's no chance that a few hundred years of selecting breeding has had any effect whatsoever on today's "domestic" horse. That 28,000 year old horse is genetically the same as the horse in your backyard. And science says that "every horse on the planet retains the ability to return successfully to the wild or feral state." Note the scientists use the word: *successfully*. In other words, today's domestic horse has the genetic ability to grow as perfect a foot and take care of himself with no help from humans every bit as well as those in the wild.

3. The horse evolved for more than 50 million years in the Great Basin of the western United States. During those millions of years he devel-

oped genetics designed to *survive* and live in a specific lifestyle in a specific manner. To eat in a specific way. To move a specific amount. To socialize in a way that provides for a specific need. The domestic horse of today retains those genetics which program his lifestyle to:

a. Move a minimum of eight to twenty miles every day of his life in search of food, water, and staying ahead of predators. Living in a stall without this movement causes both physical and mental stress to the horse, and stress, as we humans know, results in illness, organ failures, and shortened life. Also, that eight to twenty miles a day of movement helps circulate blood, is a vital part of the digestive process, and, of course, it helps the horse stay physically fit and mentally alert.

b. Eat tiny bits of forage – mostly *grass* forage – a little at a time, virtually around the clock; a minimum of 16-18 hours a day, or more. Horse tummies are tiny and not meant to eat two or three large meals a day, and their hindgut *requires* the constant passage of small amounts of *grass* forage through it in order to perform and digest as designed. Digestive acid is continually flowing, unlike in humans where digestive acid stops and starts depending upon the presence of food. In the equine hindgut it never stops. And it needs continual grass forages to wok on or it will go to work on the hindgut itself. In other words, the horse needs *free choice* grass forage or grass hay available 24/7. And their physical structure is designed to eat from the ground. Bad things happen when they don't.

c. Live within a herd. For safety, not for fun. There is safety in numbers. Separation from the herd creates emotional stress, and emotional stress attacks the physical body, and, as mentioned above, bad things happen.

d. Horses ingest very, very little sugar in the wild. Almost none. And when I say sugar I don't just mean raw sugar, candy or molasses. I mean anything that turns to sugar when it enters the body, which includes corn, oats – most grains actually – and of course molasses – even (are you ready) carrots. And some grasses. And remember your horse spent millions and

millions of years evolving... without
such sugars.

Is any of this a surprise to anyone? It certainly was to
me. A big one. These truths quite simply upended everything I thought I knew, and virtually everything I was
being told by the experienced and the qualified.

But God and Mother Nature knew what they were
doing. Horses were designed over time through trial
and error to live and eat and move in certain ways; and
the study of all of this can provide more incredibly valuable information about how we should be feeding,
keeping, and caring for the horses we choose to associ-
ate with than has ever been understood before. If it
hadn't worked so well we would've never heard of the
horse. They're a prey animal. They'd be extinct.

This ran so counter to everything I felt for my
horses. Sometimes we humans can't help ourselves. We
want to coddle and cuddle them in our terms. We want
to think of them as big dogs, and treat them in the
same manner.

They aren't big dogs.

Not even close.

Dogs, like humans, are cave dwellers. Predators,
who feel comfortable taking care of themselves. They
run in packs primarily to gain advantage in the hunt,
not for safety. Pat Parelli says humans and dogs are
most interested in *praise, recognition, and material things.*
Horses are not interested in any of that. Horses are in-

terested in *safety, emotional comfort, play, food and procre-ation*. Praise, recognition, and material things are of no interest to them. At all.

Hard to grasp, isn't it?

But, come on, what harm can it do to show a bit of TLC by storing them away in a nice comfy stall, with central heat and air, a bit of velvet on the walls, and a soft, cushy floor?

A lot of harm. Believe me when I tell you: a lot.

What we humans feel our sweet babies should have is most often exactly the opposite of what they need for health and happiness.

Again, a horse's entire physiology has been built over millions of years to:

- ✓ Move that minimum of 15 to 20 miles a day, on bare hooves
- ✓ Be with the herd, physically and thus emotionally safe, unstressed
- ✓ Spend 16 to 18 hours a day eating… from the ground, a variety but 85% to 90% grass forage, continuous uptake in small quantities to suit their small tummies and hind guts
- ✓ Control their own thermoregulatory system, thus controlling their own internal body temperature with no outside assistance, including heat, blankets, and the like

✓ Stand and walk on firm fresh ground,
not in the chemical remnants of their
own poop and pee… nor be breathing
the fumes of those remnants, plus the
excessive carbon dioxide that accumu-
lates inside a closed structure

✓ Get a certain amount of unstressed
REM sleep, which usually will only happen when surrounded by a herd with a
sentry on guard

The information was in. The undeniable truths. So how
in the world were we going to be able to meet the requirements of the horse on our tiny piece of very steep
rocks and dirt. How was I going to be able to give Cash
as good a life as I had promised. The prospect seemed
daunting if not completely impossible. That is, until the
next time I saw Cash and was reminded of that promise. And what the stalls, shoes, and sugar were doing to
his well being.

I had no choice but to figure it out.

I won't bore you with the micro steps because every
piece of property, every situation, every group of horses
are all different and the process should be approached
based upon each individual situation. Suffice to say, the
object was to accomplish the following as quickly (and
inexpensively) as possible:

• Get the shoes off of all our horses and find
someone who truly understood the reasons

and requirements of the wild horse trim (See the eBook Nugget *Why Our Horses Are Barefoot*).

- Get the horses out of their stalls 24/7, and get them moving as much as possible.
- Provide them with free-choice <u>grass</u> hay, around the clock, so they can "graze" anytime the want or need to, just as they would in the wild.

The more I've studied all this the more I have come to the conclusion that if one aspect of the wild horse lifestyle could be isolated *movement* would likely be the most important. That cannot be done of course. One aspect of their lifestyle cannot be separated from the others. It's like a jigsaw puzzle. All the pieces are related to each other. But from our own personal observation I can tell you that movement alone accomplishes so much in terms of blood circulation, digestion, muscular and skeletal issues, and stress reduction. And all of that contributes to building a strong immune system. Movement, movement, movement.

As we approached the problem of what to do we were not even considering our two and a half acre hillside behind the house. That was way too scary. We were focusing upon two "almost" paddocks on the hillside just below the stalls, both nothing but rocks and dirt and like the bigger hill behind the house both very steep. A small amount of additional fencing would close off the area and divide it into two paddocks each barely larger than the footprint of a normal size barn.

Certainly bigger than a stall, but did I say *steep?*

It seems silly as I write this, but back then we were actually afraid the horses couldn't take care of themselves on such a steep rocky hill.

"Isn't that the way they live in the wild," Kathleen asked.

"Well, yeah... but...but..."

"But what?"

I couldn't answer. My emotions were overriding my brain. I was beginning to sound like a lady we knew who had commented on what we were doing.

Oh my, shouldn't a horse pasture be flat, without any dangerous obstacles?

You mean boring?

Well, on steep rocky hills a horse might get hurt.

Tell me about it!

So it is dangerous.
The horses prefer to call it interesting.
Oh my.

Actually, the steep hills and rocks turned out to be good for the horses' bare feet, teaching them to pay attention to where they're stepping, which translates well to the trail. The level of exercise is better, thus circulation and muscle tone is better, and stamina is improved.

When the time came, Cash was first. I swung open the gate to his stall and he bolted into a dead run down the steepest of the hills, skidding to a beautiful slide stop at the bottom. He looked back up the hill and I swear he was smiling. Then he raced off into the second paddock.

In short, even though the space was really not very big, they all loved it. We accomplished the constant movement by placing free-choice hay in small piles all around the perimeter of each paddock. When horses graze, by nature, they eat a bit then take a couple of steps. If the hay is scattered in small piles, they'll do the same. The next pile always seems better than the one they're munching. *The grass is always greener...*

Add in the normal herd dynamic – we call it musical hay piles - wherein the leader is always moving the herd members along, certain that they have found something better than he has.

After observing them for a while we split the herd into two bands of three horses each because all six would invariably congregate in the same paddock and we felt that that each paddock was a bit too small – too much snotty pants - for all six at once.

We fed twice a day. A few supplements top dressed over a small dollop of Triple Crown Safe Starch forage-

in-a-bag (by this time we had ceased to feed any pro-
cessed pelleted feed. Most are very high in sugar, either
from molasses or from being grain-based, or both. Oats
and corn are way too high in non-structured carbohy-
drates – sugar – for any horse) We added a tiny bit of
alfalfa and orchard for diversity to the free choice Bermuda grass hay. To us, free-choice means: *Put out as
much as we think they'll eat in a 12-hour period. If there is
none left over we'll put out a bit more next time. If there is
some left over, we'll cut it back a bit next time.*

We quickly discovered they were eating more at
night than during the day. Especially during the sum-
mer. So we adjusted accordingly. Which is another
worthwhile point. We are continually adjusting. Anytime we see a way to do it better, or a need overlooked,
we make a change.

The photos above scattered through this section
are from our herd's brief stay in these smaller paddocks.
Brief because now that we knew they were handling the
rocks and hills with ease we began to study the possibility of doing something with the unused, going-to-waste
two-and-a-half acre hillside behind the house. And
whereas it seemed pretty much worthless for any other
use, as a natural pasture it would seriously replicate the
kind of terrain where their ancestors evolved. In that
respect it seemed perfect. At least about an acre-and-a-
half of it seemed perfect. We decided to go for it.

4
STEEP AND STEEPER

The hillside was already enclosed by a chain link fence. So we inscribed a perimeter, an oblong circle, for our "Paddock Paradise" within that square (the outside circle of dots in the photo below - yellow in the color eBook version) and put up an electric fence using Premier1 electric braid rope and t-posts. I installed it myself in a matter of a few days. Well... okay, maybe a week.

Then we inscribed an inner circle (blue dots in the color photo) and, again, installed the electric rope and t-post fence. The purpose of the inner circle was: 1) to extend the overall length of the "track" by forcing the horses to make the entire circle, removing the possibility that any horse could "cheat" by cutting across the center. The center was in effect a "no fly zone"... and... 2) the center was mostly huge, slippery, steep boulders which we felt were too dangerous to leave to the horses' discretion (there's that human resistance to trust the horse again).

The outer dots are the perimeter
The inner dots the "no fly zone"

Now it was time to try it.

We were worried.

Was it too steep? Would the horses like it? Were there too many rocks and boulders? Would they hurt themselves? Would they all get along in the same pasture?

Scribbles was first.

He's the quiet one. A gorgeous paint, but charisma is not his long suit. He's the one most likely to be found standing in a corner, motionless, seemingly, for hours. Lazy would be a merciful understatement. He has the best *whoa* of any of our six, because it's his favorite speed. No reins needed. Just sit back a little, then hold on for the screech of tires. *Can we stop now?* is his favorite question. He leads like it's an imposition to ask him to move. *Oh all right, if you insist, but you have no idea how much effort this is.*

Which is why his first venture into the natural pasture left me with my mouth hanging open in astonishment. As the halter fell away, he spun and was gone like a bullet. Racing, kicking the air, tossing his head, having the best time I'd ever seen him have. This was not a horse I had met before. He went on for a good ten minutes, with me just standing there, grinning like an idiot.

I could imagine that somewhere inside those two brains he was screeching *Whoopee! I'm free! I'm free!* Finally, he trotted back over and in his own begrudging little way said thank-you. That was the beginning of a new way of life for Scribbles and his five herd mates.

The morning and evening feeds were very much like the smaller paddocks except now the hay piles around the circle covered more ground and numbered over 100. We were mixing in the small amounts of orchard and alfalfa all the way around because we found that the herd would go around once for the alfalfa, then again for the orchard, then again for the Bermuda, then again to clean up the dregs.

After a mid-day nap they'd take a couple more spins all the way around. We estimated that, on average, they were traveling approximately eight to ten miles in a twenty-four hour day.

Kathleen and I spent hours sitting on a big, hard rock watching our herd investigate their new world. The horses paraded from the north end to the south, frolicked and played and moved each other around. They ran up and down the hill, nibbled on stray weeds, and otherwise had a fine time being out in the wild, so to speak. They were finally home. And their health and happiness blossomed.

On the very last day that we lived on this property before moving from "no" grasses to the "rich" grasses of middle Tennessee (See the Book *Horses Were Born To Be On Grass)* it occurred to Kathleen that we had not recorded the entire process on video. And so she did. Perhaps now is the time to take a look. Just go to The Soul of a Horse Channel on YouTube: *Our Paddock Paradise: What We Did. How We Did It. And Why?*

As the logic of all this and how beautifully it was working sank in, Kathleen and I often found ourselves looking at each other through astonished eyes. Either our discoveries were truly amazing, or we were certifiably nuts. How could so many people be so wrong for so long? It simply didn't make any sense.

"But we began the same way," Kathleen said one day. "We were right there, buying into the stalls, the shoes, the sugar."

She was right. When we began this journey, I'm not even sure we realized that wild horses still existed. We certainly didn't know that they had been around for fifty-two million years. So, like most people, we had given no thought to how they had survived all that time with no assistance from humans. We simply had no knowledge of any of it, so how could it apply to us? Which, unfortunately, is the case with most of the folks we've run into.

Now, when we start spewing all this information at some unsuspecting horse owner, eyes widen and jaws drop. And some of them rush off to get away from the weirdos.

But many of them rush off to be pardoned by their horses. Some of their stories are on our website. On The Soul of a Horse website, scroll down and click on: No Stalls, No Shoes, No Sugar. These stories make it all worth every effort.

To build a natural pasture yourself is way easier than you might think (if I can do it anyone can do it!). Often, depending upon how many horses you have, you need little more room than required for a barn (See the Resources at the end of the book). I have seen a Paddock Paradise as small as 60' x 60', with back and forth tracks like those mazes we used to draw as kids stretching the length of "track" to nearly 500 hundred feet. Whatever your situation might be, you can figure something out that's better than being cooped up in a stall.

When we take control of one of these lives, when we say *I will be responsible for this animal, his care and feeding, his health and happiness,* we tacitly promise to give him the very best care that we can. To learn everything we can about the horse, and how to give him the longest and very best life possible. Not the life *we* think he should have because that's what *we'd* like, but the life we *know* is right because we've studied it and *are certain.*

Cash is by far our most accident prone horse. Giving me every excuse in the world to not allow him (or any other horse) out on such a steep rocky hillside. He pulled a tendon recently and had to be confined. And oh how he hated it. I sometimes want to put him in a padded room to keep him from hurting himself, wrap him up in a thick fuzzy blanket. Feed him warm tea and hot chocolate. But watching him pace in his stall awakens me from this human delusion. I have never forgotten how happy he was when he was first turned loose in the big natural pasture. The smile on his face. The prancing. The racing. The kicking. He was eleven hundred pounds of pure frolic.

So, of course, I had no choice but to let him go back as soon as he was better.

Because I had a promise to keep.

And because I love him.

It was late afternoon and Kathleen and I were once again sitting on our front porch looking out over the cute white stalls with the red roofs. The sun was sinking beneath the ridge of mountains to the west.

"Those stalls surely seem empty," Kathleen said. "Wouldn't it be nice if there were a couple of horses ambling back and forth down there?"

"Those were the days," I said.

"Like a picture postcard."

We both smiled.

"Too bad it didn't work out. I enjoyed watching them."

"Yeah," Kathleen said. "Too bad."

"It's hard to believe we were so stupid."

"Not stupid," she corrected. "Lacking knowledge."

"That was a long time ago."

"Coming up on two years," she chuckled, and raised her wineglass to mine. They clinked softly.

"We done good," she said. "We done good."

Follow Joe & Kathleen's Journey

From no horses and no clue to stumbling through mistakes, fear, fascination and frustration on a collision course with the ultimate discovery that something was very wrong in the world of horses.

Read the National Best Seller
The Soul of a Horse
Life Lessons from the Herd

…and the highly acclaimed best selling sequel…

Born Wild
The Soul of a Horse

Go to: www.thesoulofahorse.com

The above links and all of the links that follow are live links in the eBook editions and all photos are in color. Available at Amazon Kindle, Barnes & Noble Nook and Apple iBooks

WHAT READERS AND CRITICS ARE SAYING ABOUT JOE CAMP

"Joe Camp is a master storyteller." *THE NEW YORK TIMES*

"Joe Camp is a gifted storyteller and the results are magical. Joe entertains, educates and empowers, baring his own soul while articulating keystone principles of a modern revolution in horsemanship." *RICK LAMB, AUTHOR AND TV/RADIO HOST "THE HORSE SHOW"*

"This book is fantastic. It has given me shivers, made me laugh and cry, and I just can't seem to put it down!" *CHERYL PANNIER, WHO RADIO AM 1040 DES MOINES*

"One cannot help but be touched by Camp's love and sympathy for animals and by his eloquence on the subject." *MICHAEL KORDA, THE WASHINGTON POST*

"Joe Camp is a natural when it comes to understanding how animals tick and a genius at telling us their story. His books are must-reads for those who love animals of any species." *MONTY ROBERTS, AUTHOR OF NEW YORK TIMES BEST-SELLER THE MAN WHO LISTENS TO HORSES*

"Camp has become something of a master at telling us what can be learned from animals, in this case specifically horses, without making us realize we have been educated, and, that is, perhaps, the mark of a real teacher. The tightly written, simply designed, and powerfully drawn chapters often read like short stories that flow from the heart." *JACK L. KENNEDY, THE JOPLIN INDEPENDENT*

"This book is absolutely fabulous! An amazing, amazing book. You're going to love it." *JANET PARSHALL'S AMERICA*

"Joe speaks a clear and simple truth that grabs hold of your heart." *YVONNE WELZ, EDITOR, THE HORSE'S HOOF MAGAZINE*

"I wish you could *hear* my excitement for Joe Camp's new book. It is unique, powerful, needed." *DR. MARTY BECKER, BEST-SELLING AUTHOR OF SEVERAL CHICKEN SOUP FOR THE SOUL BOOKS AND POPULAR VETERINARY CONTRIBUTOR TO ABC'S GOOD MORNING AMERICA*

"I got my book yesterday and hold Joe Camp responsible for my bloodshot eyes. I couldn't put it down and morning came early!!! Joe transports me into his words. I feel like I am right there sharing his experiences. And his love for not just horses, but all of God's critters pours out from every page." *RUTH SWANDER – READER*

"I love this book! It is so hard to put it down, but I also don't want to read it too fast. I don't want it to end! Every person who loves an animal must have this book. I can't wait for the next one !!!!!!!!!" *NINA BLACK REID – READER*

"I LOVED the book! I had it read in 2 days. I had to make myself put it down. Joe and Kathleen have brought so much light to how horses should be treated and cared for. Again, thank you!" *ANITA LARGE - READER*

"LOVE the new book… reading it was such an emotional journey. Joe Camp is a gifted writer." *MARYKAY THUL LONGACRE - READER*

"I was actually really sad, when I got to the last page, because I was looking forward to picking it up every night." SABINE REYNOSO - READER

"*The Soul of a Horse Blogged* is insightful, enlightening, emotionally charged, hilarious, packed with wonderfully candid photography, and is masterfully woven by a consummate storyteller. Wonderful reading!" HARRY H. MACDONALD - READER

"I simply love the way Joe Camp writes. He stirs my soul. This is a must read book for everyone." *DEBBIE K - READER*

"This book swept me away. From the first to last page I felt transported! It's clever, witty, inspiring and a very fast read. I was sad when I finished it because I wanted to read more!" *DEBBIE CHARTRAND – READER*

"This book is an amazing, touching insight into Joe and Kathleen's personal journey that has an even more intimate feel than Joe's first best seller." *KATHERINE BOWEN – READER*

Also by Joe Camp

The National Best Seller
The Soul of a Horse
Life Lessons from the Herd

The Highly Acclaimed Best Selling Sequel
Born Wild
The Soul of a Horse

Horses & Stress
Eliminating the Root Cause of Most Health, Hoof & Behavior Problems

Why Relationship First Works
Why and How It Changes Everything

Beginning Ground Work
Everything We've Learned About Relationship and Leadership

Training with Treats
*With Relationship and Basic Training Locked In Treats Can Be
an Excellent Way to Enhance Good Communication*

God Only Knows
Can You Trust Him with the Secret?

Why Our Horses Are Barefoot
*Everything We've Learned About the
Health and Happiness of the Hoof*

The Soul of a Horse Blogged
The Journey Continues

Horses Were Born To Be On Grass
*How We Discovered the Simple But Undeniable Truth About Grass, Sugar,
Equine Diet & Lifestyle*

Who Needs Hollywood
The Amazing Story of How Benji Became the #3 Movie of the Year

Dog On It
Everything You Need To Know About Life Is Right There At Your Feet

RESOURCES

There are, I'm certain, many programs and people who subscribe to these philosophies and are very good at what they do but are not listed in these resources. That's because we haven't experienced them, and we will only recommend to you programs that we believe, from our own personal experience, to be good for the horse and well worth the time and money.

Monty Roberts and Join up:
http://www.montyroberts.com- Please start here! Or at Monty's Equus Online University which is terrific and probably the best Equine learning value out there on the internet (Watch the Join-Up lesson <u>and</u> the Special Event lesson. Inspiring!). This is where you get the relationship right with your horse. Where you learn to give him the choice of whether or not to trust you. Where everything changes when he does. Please, do this. Learn Monty's Join-Up method, either from his Online University, his books, or DVDs. Watching his *Join-Up* DVD was probably our single most pivotal experience in our very short journey with horses. Even if you've owned your horse forever, go back to the beginning and execute a Join Up with your horse or horses. You'll find that when you unconditionally offer choice to your horse and he chooses you, everything changes. You become a member of the herd, and your horse's

leader, and with that goes responsibility on his part as well as yours. Even if you don't own horses, it is absolutely fascinating to watch Monty put a saddle and a rider on a completely unbroken horse in less than thirty minutes (unedited!). We've also watched and used Monty's *Dually Training Halter* DVD and his *Load-Up trailering* DVD. And we loved his books: *The Man Who Listens to Horses, The Horses in My Life, From My Hands to Yours, and Shy Boy*. Monty is a very impressive man who cares a great deal for horses.

http://www.imagineahorse.com- This is Allen Pogue and Suzanne De Laurentis' site. I cannot recommend strongly enough that everyone who leaves this eBook Nugget ready to take the next step with treats and vocabulary should visit this site and start collecting Allen's DVDs (he also sells big red circus balls). Because of his liberty work with multiple horses Allen has sort of been cast as a trick trainer, but he's so much more than that. It's all about relationship and foundation. We are dumbfounded by how Allen's horses treat him and try for him. His work with newborn foals and young horses is so logical and powerful that you should study it even if you never intend to own a horse. Allen says, "With my young horses, by the time they are three years old they are so mentally mature that saddling and riding is absolutely undramatic." He has taken Dr. Robert M.

Miller's book *Imprint Training of the Newborn Foal* to a new and exponential level.

Frederick Pignon – This man is amazing and has taken relationship and bond with his horses to an astounding new level. Go to this link: (http://www.youtube.com/watch?v=w1YO3j-Zh3g) and watch the video of his show with three beautiful black Lusitano stallions, all at liberty. This show would border on the miraculous if they were all geldings, but they're not. They're stallions. Most of us will never achieve the level of bond Frederick has achieved with his horses but it's inspiring to know that it's possible, and to see what the horse-human relationship is capable of becoming. Frederick believes in true partnership with his horses, he believes in making every training session fun not work, he encourages the horses to offer their ideas, and he uses treats. When Kathleen read his book *Gallop to Freedom* her response to me was simply, "Can we just move in with them?"

<u>Natural Horsemanship</u>: This is the current buzz word for those who train horses or teach humans the training of horses without any use of fear, cruelty, threats, aggression, or pain. The philosophy is growing like wildfire, and why shouldn't it? If you can accomplish everything you could ever hope for with your horse and still have a terrific relationship with him or her, and be re-

spected as a leader, not feared as a dominant predator, why wouldn't you? As with any broadly based general philosophy, there are many differing schools of thought on what is important and what isn't, what works well and what doesn't. Which of these works best for you, I believe, depends a great deal on how you learn, and how much reinforcement and structure you need. In our beginnings, we more or less shuffled together Monty Roberts (above) and the next two whose websites are listed below, favoring one source for this and another for that. But beginning with Monty's Join-Up. Often, this gave us an opportunity to see how different programs handle the same topic, which enriches insight. But, ultimately, they all end up at the same place: When you have a good relationship with your horse that began with choice, when you are respected as your horse's leader, when you truly care for your horse, then, before too long, you will be able to figure out for yourself the best communication to evoke any particular objective. These programs, as written, or taped on DVD, merely give you a structured format to follow that will take you to that goal.

http://www.parelli.com- Pat and Linda Parelli have turned their teaching methods into a fully accredited college curriculum. We have four of their home DVD courses: *Level 1, Level 2, Level 3,* and *Liberty & Horse Behavior.* We recommend them all, but especially the first three. Often, they do run on, dragging out points much longer than perhaps necessary, but we've found, particularly in the early days, that knowledge gained through such saturation always bubbles up to present itself at the most opportune moments. In other words, it's good. Soak it up. It'll pay dividends later. Linda is a good instructor, especially in the first three programs, and Pat is one of the most amazing horsemen I've ever seen. His antics are inspirational for me. Not that I will ever duplicate any of them, but knowing that it's possible is very affirming. And watching him with a newborn foal is just fantastic. The difficulty for us with *Liberty & Horse Behavior* (besides its price) is on disk 5 whereon Linda consumes almost three hours to load an inconsistent horse into a trailer. Her belief is that the horse should *not* be *made* to do anything, he should *discover* it on his own. I believe there's another option. As Monty Roberts teaches, there is a big difference between *making* a horse do something and *leading* him through it, showing him that it's okay, that his trust in you is valid. Once you have joined up with him, and he trusts you, he is willing to take chances for you because of that trust, so long as you don't abuse the trust. On Monty's trailer-loading DVD Monty takes about one-tenth the time, and the horse (who was impossible to load before Monty) winds up loading himself from thirty feet away, happily, even playfully. And his trust in Monty has progressed as well, because he reached beyond his comfort zone and learned it was okay. His trust was confirmed. One thing the Parelli program stresses, in a way, is a followup to Monty Roberts' Join-Up: you should spend a lot of time just hanging out with your horse. In the stall, in the pasture, wherever. Quality time, so to speak. No agenda, just hanging out. Very much a relationship enhancer. And don't ever stomp straight over to your horse and slap on a halter. Wait. Let your horse come to you. It's that choice thing again, and Monty or Pat and Linda Parelli can teach you how it works.

http://www.chrislombard.com/ - An amazing horseman and wonderful teacher. His DVD *Beginning with the Horse* puts relationship, leadership and trust into simple easy-to-understand terms.

http://www.downunderhorsemanship.com- This is Clinton Anderson's site. Whereas the Parellis are very philosophically oriented, Clinton gets down to business with lots of detail and repetition. What exactly do I do to get my horse to back up? From the ground and from the saddle, he shows you precisely, over and over again. And when you're in the arena or round pen and forget whether he used his left hand or right hand, or whether his finger was pointing up or down, it's very easy to go straightaway to the answer on his DVDs. His programs are very task-oriented, and, again, there are a bunch of them. We have consumed his *Gaining Respect and Control on the Ground, Series I through III* and *Riding with Confidence, Series I through III.* All are multiple DVD sets, so there has been a lot of viewing and reviewing. For the most part, his tasks and the Parellis are much the same, though usually approached very differently. Both have served a purpose for us. We also loved his *No Worries Tying DVD* for use with his Australian Tie Ring, which truly eliminates pull-back problems in minutes! And on this one he demonstrates terrific desensitizing techniques. Clinton is the only two-time winner of the Road to the Horse competition, in which three top natural-horsemanship clinicians are given unbroken horses and a mere three hours to be riding and performing specified tasks.

Those DVDs are terrific! And Clinton's Australian accent is also fun to listen to... mate.

The three programs above have built our natural horsemanship foundation, and we are in their debt. The following are a few others you should probably check out, each featuring a highly respected clinician, and all well known for their care and concern for horses.

http://www.robertmmiller.com - Dr. Robert M. Miller is an equine veterinarian and world renowned speaker and author on horse behavior and natural horsemanship. I think his name comes up more often in these circles than anyone else's. His first book, *Imprint Training of the Newborn Foal* is now a bible of the horse world. He's not really a trainer, per se, but a phenomenal resource on horse behavior. He will show you the route to "the bond." You must visit his website.

<u>Taking Your Horse Barefoot:</u> Taking your horses barefoot involves more than just pulling shoes. The new breed of natural hoof care practitioners have studied and rely completely on what they call the wild horse trim, which replicates the trim that horses give to themselves in the wild through natural wear. The more

the domesticated horse is out and about, moving constantly, the less trimming he or she will need. The more stall-bound the horse, the more trimming will be needed in order to keep the hooves healthy and in shape. Every horse is a candidate to live as nature intended. The object is to maintain their hooves as if they were in the wild, and that requires some study. Not a lot, but definitely some. I now consider myself capable of keeping my horses' hooves in shape. I don't do their regular trim, but I do perform interim touch-ups. The myth that domesticated horses *must* wear shoes has been proven to be pure hogwash. The fact that shoes degenerate the health of the hoof and the entire horse has not only been proven, but is also recognized even by those who nail shoes on horses. Successful high performance barefootedness with the wild horse trim can be accomplished for virtually every horse on the planet, and the process has even been proven to be a healing procedure for horses with laminitis and founder. On this subject, I beg you not to wait. Dive into the material below and give your horse a longer, healthier, happier life.

http://www.hoofrehab.com/– This is Pete Ramey's website. If you read only one book on this entire subject, read Pete's *Making Natural Hoof Care Work for You.* Or better yet, get his DVD series *Under the Horse*, which is fourteen-plus hours of terrific research, trimming, and information. He is my hero! He has had so much experience with making horses better. He cares so much about every horse that he helps. And all of this comes out in his writing and DVD series. If you've ever doubted the fact that horses do not need metal shoes and are in fact better off without them, please go to Pete's website. He will convince you otherwise. Then use his teachings to guide your horses' venture into barefootedness. He is never afraid or embarrassed to change his opinion on something as he learns more from his experiences. Pete's writings have also appeared in *Horse & Rider* and are on his website. He has taken all of Clinton Anderson's horses barefoot.

The following are other websites that contain good information regarding the barefoot subject:

http://www.TheHorsesHoof.com– this website and magazine of Yvonne and James Welz is devoted entirely to barefoot horses around the world and is surely the single largest resource for owners, trimmers, case histories, and virtually everything you would ever want to know about barefoot horses. With years and years of barefoot experience, Yvonne is an amazing resource.

She can compare intelligently this method vs that and help you to understand all there is to know. And James is a super barefoot trimmer.

http://www.wholehorsetrim.com - This is the website of Eddie Drabek, another one of my heroes. Eddie is a wonderful trimmer in Houston, Texas, and an articulate and inspirational educator and spokesman for getting metal shoes off horses. Read everything he has written, including the pieces on all the horses whose lives he has saved by taking them barefoot.

Our current hoof specialist in Tennessee is Mark Taylor who works in Tennessee, Arkansas, Alabama, and Mississippi 662-224-4158 http://www.barefoothorsetrimming.com/

http://www.aanhcp.net- This is the website for the American Association of Natural Hoof Care Practioners.

Also see: **the video of Joe: Why Are Our Horses Barefoot? On** The Soul of a Horse Channel on YouTube.

Natural Boarding: Once your horses are barefoot, please begin to figure out how to keep them out around the clock, day and night, moving constantly, or at least having that option. It's really not as difficult as you might imagine, even if you only have access to a small piece of property. Every step your horse takes makes his hooves and his body healthier, his immune system better. And it really is not that difficult or expensive to figure it out. Much cheaper than barns and stalls.

Paddock Paradise: A Guide to Natural Horse Boarding This book by Jaime Jackson begins with a study of horses in the wild, then describes many plans for getting your horses out 24/7, in replication of the wild. The designs are all very specific, but by reading the entire book you begin to deduce what's really important and what's not so important, and why. We didn't follow any of his plans, but we have one pasture that's probably an acre and a half and two much smaller ones (photos on our website www.thesoulofahorse.com). All of them function very well when combined with random food placement. They keep our horses on the move, as they would be in the wild. The big one is very inexpensively electrically-fenced. *Paddock Paradise* is available, as are all of Jaime's books, at **http://www.paddockparadise.com/**

Also see the video **The Soul of a Horse Paddock Paradise: What We Did, How We Did It, and Why** on The Soul of a Horse Channel on YouTube.

New resources are regularly updated on Kathleen's and my: **www.theSoulofaHorse.com** or our blog **http://thesoulofahorse.com/blog**

Liberated Horsemanship at:
http://www.liberatedhorsemanship.com/
Scroll down to the fifth Article in the column on the right entitled Barefoot Police Horses

An article about the Houston Mounted Patrol on our website: Houston Patrol Article

The following are links to videos on various subjects, all found on our The Soul of a Horse Channel on YouTube:

Video of Joe: Why Are Our Horses Barefoot?

Video of Joe: Why Our Horses Eat from the Ground

Video: Finding The Soul of a Horse

Video of Joe and Cash: Relationship First!

Video: The Soul of a Horse Paddock Paradise: What
We Did, How We Did It, and Why

Don't Ask for Patience – God Will Give You a Horse

The next 2 links are to very short videos of a horse's
hoof hitting the ground. One is a shod hoof, one is
barefoot. Watch the vibrations roll up the leg from the
shod hoof... then imagine that happening every time
any shod hoof hits the ground: to view go to The Soul
of a Horse Channel on YouTube:

Video: Shod Hoof
Video: Barefoot Hoof

Find a recommended trimmer in your area:

http://www.aanhcp.net

http://www.americanhoofassociation.org

http://www.pacifichoofcare.org

http://www.liberatedhorsemanship.com/

Valuable Links on Diet and Nutrition:

Dr. Juliette Getty's website:
http://gettyequinenutrition.biz/

Dr. Getty's favorite feed/forage testing facility:
http://www.equi-analytical.com

For more about pretty much anything in this book
please visit one of these websites:

www.thesoulofahorse.com

http://thesoulofahorse.com/blog

www.14handspress.com

www.thesoulofahorseblogged.com

The Soul of a Horse Fan Page on Facebook

The Soul of a Horse Channel on YouTube

Joe and The Soul of a Horse on Twitter
@Joe_Camp

Printed in Great Britain
by Amazon

65449585R00045